Name ______________________

MW01698310

Family: Children will be tested on these spelling words. Have your child read the words, write each word in a box, and cut the boxes apart. Use the word cards for spelling practice throughout the week. Choose a card, say the word, and ask your child to write it.

Spelling List

cliff	baffled	cuddle	dull	miss	tussle
spelling	press	hassle	ruffle	saddle	huddle

Name ______________________________

Family: Listen to your child read the story a few times this week. With repeated practice, the reading should become smoother and more accurate.

Green Walls

Grass isn't just for lawns. Now grass and other plants are grown on the walls of some buildings. These walls are called "green walls." Green walls help in many ways. First, plants soak up light and heat. They help keep the sun's heat from going into the building. That keeps the building cooler and saves money on air conditioning. Plants also soak up sound, which makes the building quieter inside. Green walls are great! How do you think people mow them?

© YONG KWAN KIM

Name ______________________________

Family: Have your child read the spelling words in the lists and then put each list in ABC order on the lines below.

List 1

baffled	dull
cuddle	cliff
tussle	miss

1. ____________________
2. ____________________
3. ____________________
4. ____________________
5. ____________________
6. ____________________

List 2

spelling	press
hassle	ruffle
saddle	huddle

1. ____________________
2. ____________________
3. ____________________
4. ____________________
5. ____________________
6. ____________________

Name ______________________________

Family: Have your child complete the spelling words by tracing the grey letters and writing in the missing double letters *ff*, *dd*, *ll*, or *ss*.

ff **dd** **ll** **ss**

1.	s	p	e			i	n	g
2.	c	l	i					
3.	b	a			l	e	d	
4.	p	r	e					
5.	s	a			l	e		
6.	r	u			l	e		
7.	m	i						
8.	d	u						
9.	c	u			l	e		
10.	h	a			l	e		
11.	h	u			l	e		
12.	t	u			l	e		

Name ______________________________

Family: Have your child read the recipe. You can then follow the directions to make the snack together.

Orange Cups

You will need:

- a cutting board
- paper towel
- an orange
- fruit cocktail or fruit salad
- coconut flakes
- a small plate

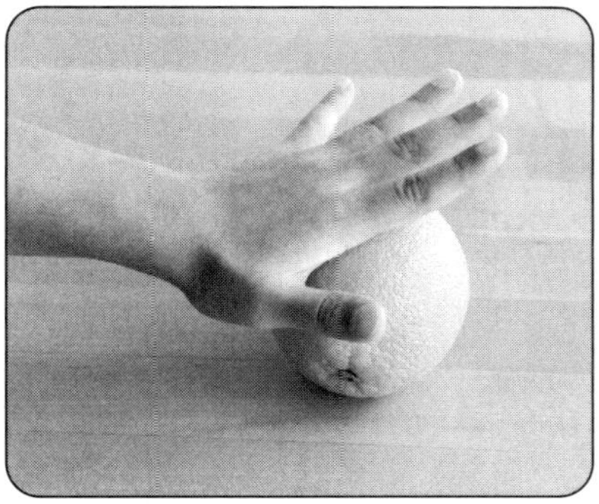

1. PUT the orange on a cutting board. Press down on the orange and roll it. This will make it easier to scoop out. Now ask an adult to cut the orange in half.

2. USE a spoon to scrape the fruit out of the peel onto the cutting board. Save the peel. It will be your cup.

3. SPLIT the orange pieces and put them in a bowl. Add fruit cocktail and stir.

4. FILL your orange cup with the fruit mix.

STEVEN TALLEY/TALLEY PHOTO

5. SPRINKLE coconut over the fruit cup. Set your cup on a plate and serve your dish with a-peel!

Backpack Page 6

Unit 9, Spelling

Name ______________________________

Family: Children will be tested on these spelling words. Have your child read the words, write each word in a box, and cut the boxes apart. Use the word cards for spelling practice throughout the week. Choose a card, say the word, and ask your child to write it.

Spelling List

above	against	amount	happen	kitten	ribbon
adult	America	apart	children	button	cotton

Name ______________________________

Family: Listen to your child read the story a few times this week. With repeated practice, the reading should become smoother and more accurate.

Pretty in Pink

You probably haven't seen a pink dolphin before. Pink dolphins are rare. Most dolphins are gray. This little dolphin is pink because it is an albino (say it: al-BY-no). That means the dolphin is missing pigment in its skin that would make it a darker color. Pigment would make the dolphin's skin gray. Humans and other animals can be albinos too. Albino animals and people often have pale skin and white fur or hair. Their eyes can be pink or blue.

ZUMA PRESS/NEWSCOM

Name ______________________

Family: Have your child write the missing spelling word to complete each phrase.

Spelling List

above	against	amount	happen	kitten	ribbon
adult	America	apart	children	button	cotton

1. A__________ the beautiful
2. b__________ your coat
3. a__________ or together
4. a__________ or child
5. k__________ or puppy
6. h__________ now or later
7. c__________ or adults
8. r__________ in your hair
9. a__________ or for
10. a__________ or below
11. a__________ to be paid
12. c__________ candy

Name ______________________________

Family: Have your child write missing letters to complete the spelling words in the puzzles.

Spelling List

- ☐ cotton
- ☐ above
- ☐ against
- ☐ apart
- ☐ America
- ☐ kitten
- ☐ adult
- ☐ ribbon
- ☐ children
- ☐ button
- ☐ happen
- ☐ amount

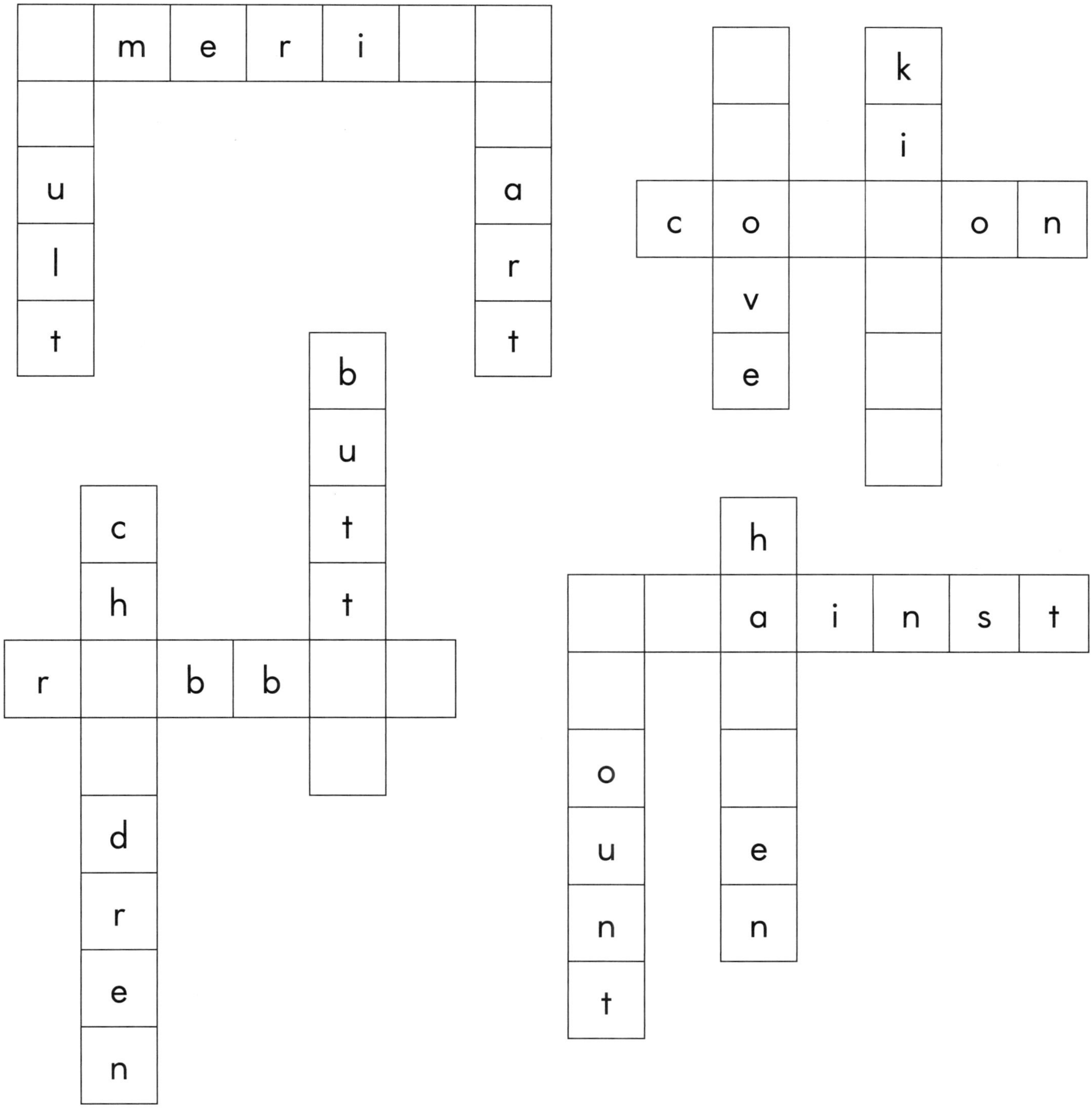

Name ______________________________

Family: Children will be tested on these spelling words. Have your child read the words, write each word in a box, and cut the boxes apart. Use the word cards for spelling practice throughout the week. Choose a card, say the word, and ask your child to write it.

Spelling List

delay	okay	weight	neighbor	strange	danger
maybe	dismay	eighteen	eighty	change	ranger

Name ______________________________

Family: Listen to your child read the story a few times this week. With repeated practice, the reading should become smoother and more accurate.

Poor Oswald?

One of the things the Superkids loved most about second grade was Book Club. In Book Club, they got to read real chapter books with Ms. Blossom. Sometimes they did a project in class about the book they were reading. Sometimes they did homework.

Today, Ms. Blossom said, "Who would like to share their Book Club homework?"

Tac raised her hand. She saw Oswald trying to smooth his paper, which was wet and wrinkled. Smoothing it was a mistake, because he smeared his drawing.

Ms. Blossom picked up Oswald's paper. "May I share your work?" she asked.

Oswald nodded unhappily. "OK," he said.

Poor Oswald, thought Tac. Ms. Blossom was always kind, but Tac was sure she'd say that Oswald's work was messy.

"Class," said Ms. Blossom. "Look at Oswald's horse. It is blurry and tilted, so we can tell that it is running downhill fast. Oswald's handwriting is slanted, so that the way the words look shows what they mean." Ms. Blossom smiled at Oswald. "Your work gives us a feeling of speed and excitement. It's splendid."

"Thanks!" said Oswald. He grinned at Tac as if to say, "Phew!"

Name ______________________________

Family: Have your child write the spelling word that answers each question.

Spelling List

delay	okay	weight	neighbor	strange	danger
maybe	dismay	eighteen	eighty	change	ranger

1. Which two words begin and end like day? ____________ ____________
2. Which word begins and ends like roar? ____________
3. Which word begins and ends like charge? ____________
4. Which word begins and ends like empty? ____________
5. Which word begins and ends like near? ____________
6. Which word begins and ends like make? ____________
7. Which word begins and ends like obey? ____________
8. Which word begins and ends like wait? ____________
9. Which word begins and ends like even? ____________
10. Which word begins and ends like stage? ____________
11. Which word begins and ends like dancer? ____________

Name ______________________________

Family: Have your child complete two spelling words to match each clue. The first answer is provided. The two words will have the same long *a* spelling in them.

Spelling List

delay	okay	weight	neighbor	strange	danger
maybe	dismay	eighteen	eighty	change	ranger

1. It could be all right.

   maybe ______ okay ______

2. odd coins

   s ______ c ______

3. how heavy someone who lives by you is

   n ______ 's w ______

4. to wait to feel unhappy

   de ______ di ______

5. 80 + 18

   e ______ plus e ______

6. what a fire fighter faces

   r ______ d ______

Name ___________________________

Family: Children will be tested on these spelling words. Have your child read the words, write each word in a box, and cut the boxes apart. Use the word cards for spelling practice throughout the week. Choose a card, say the word, and ask your child to write it.

Spelling List

key	money	piece	believe	machine	marine
turkey	honey	chief	achieve	magazine	gasoline

Name ________________________________

Family: Listen to your child read the story a few times this week. With repeated practice, the reading should become smoother and more accurate.

Hair Combs

"What's that big lump in your backpack?" Icky asked Sal as they were riding the bus to the museum on Friday afternoon.

"It's my, um, my pajamas," said Sal. He quickly pointed to Lily. "Look who brought a pillow! What a baby!"

"I know," agreed Icky. "Can you believe her pillowcase has brides on it? Yuck!"

"Hey, Lily," called Sal. "Knock, knock."

"Who's there?" said Lily.

"Hair combs," said Sal.

"Hair combs who?" said Lily.

"Hair combs the bride!" said Sal.

"Yes," teased Icky. "And she's all over your pillowcase!"

Icky and Sal laughed and laughed.

Lily was annoyed.

"Don't pay any attention to them," Cass said to her. "You were smart to bring a pillow."

Lily smiled at Cass. "Let's put our sleeping bags next to each other tonight," she said. "You can share my pillow if you want."

"Thanks!" said Cass.

Name ________________________________

Family: Have your child find and circle each spelling word in the word-search puzzle and check it off in the list. The words are hidden across and up and down.

Spelling List

- ☐ key
- ☐ believe
- ☐ turkey
- ☐ achieve
- ☐ money
- ☐ machine
- ☐ honey
- ☐ magazine
- ☐ piece
- ☐ marine
- ☐ chief
- ☐ gasoline

g	a	s	o	l	i	n	e	a	m
t	b	p	i	e	c	e	k	c	a
u	m	a	r	i	n	e	e	h	g
r	c	h	o	n	e	y	y	i	a
k	d	e	m	n	o	p	s	e	z
e	b	e	l	i	e	v	e	v	i
y	g	m	o	n	e	y	a	e	n
k	i	d	m	a	c	h	i	n	e
s	t	u	r	k	e	v	e	r	y
c	h	i	e	f	i	k	l	t	u

Name ______________________________

Family: Have your child circle the spelling word in each group of letters, write the word on the lines by the matching number, and then write in order the extra letters to discover the last line to the knock-knock joke at the bottom of the page.

1. y k e y
2. c h i e f o
3. u m a c h i n e
4. r m a g a z i n e
5. m o n e y e
6. w t u r k e y
7. m a g a z i n e e
8. b e l i e v e l
9. m a r i n e c
10. g a s o l i n e o
11. m p i e c e
12. e a c h i e v e

1. ____________________
2. ____________________
3. ____________________
4. ____________________
5. ____________________
6. ____________________
7. ____________________
8. ____________________
9. ____________________
10. ____________________
11. ____________________
12. ____________________

Knock knock!
Who's there?
Tank!
Tank who?
Answer: ___ ___ ___' ___ ___ ___ ___ ___ ___ ___ ___ ___!
1 2 3 4 5 6 7 8 9 10 11 12

Name ______________________________

Family: Children will be tested on these spelling words. Have your child read the words, write each word in a box, and cut the boxes apart. Use the word cards for spelling practice throughout the week. Choose a card, say the word, and ask your child to write it.

Spelling List

planning	sitting	writing	jogged	scrubbed	smiled
swimming	making	giggling	stopped	agreed	decided

Name ______________________________

Family: Listen to your child read the story a few times this week. With repeated practice, the reading should become smoother and more accurate.

Through the Woods

It's safe to drive a car into a tree! Of course, it must be the right kind of tree. Giant redwood trees in California are some of the largest trees on earth. A few of these trees have been made into drive-through trees. A drive-through tree is a giant tree with a hole cut in its trunk. The tree is still alive. People cut the holes to attract visitors. Every day, people pay to drive their cars through these amazing trees.

ANDY RYAN/GETTY IMAGES

Name ______________________________

Family: Have your child subtract and add letters to write a spelling word that solves each word problem. Explain that the new letters should be added in the same place where letters were taken away. The first problem has been completed.

1. plan + n + ing = planning
2. make – e + ing = ______________
3. stop + p + ed = ______________
4. smile + d = ______________
5. write – e + ing = ______________
6. sit + t + ing = ______________
7. jog + g + ed = ______________
8. agree + d = ______________
9. swim + m + ing = ______________
10. decide + d = ______________
11. giggle – e + ing = ______________
12. scrub + b + ed = ______________

Name ________________________________

Family: Have your child read the spelling words at the top of the page, then unscramble the words and write each word correctly on the line. The ending of each word has been provided.

unscrmable

Spelling List

planning	sitting	writing	jogged
scrubbed	smiled	swimming	making
giggling	stopped	agreed	decided

1. lannp ____________ing
2. ppsto ____________ed
3. areg ____________ed
4. igggl ____________ing
5. lsmi ____________ed
6. bbscru ____________ed
7. istt ____________ing
8. wrti ____________ing
9. ggjo ____________ed
10. kam ____________ing
11. wimms ____________ing
12. dceid ____________ed

Name ________________________________

Family: Have your child read the recipe. You can then follow the directions to make the snack together.

Ant Farm

You will need:

- a plastic zipper bag
- 4 graham crackers
- a clear cup or glass
- a spoon
- vanilla yogurt (6 ounces)
- chocolate sprinkles

1. PUT the graham crackers into the plastic bag. Zip the bag. Crush the crackers into crumbs with your hands. The crumbs will be the dirt in your ant farm dessert.

2. POUR a layer of crumbs into the glass. Then drop some sprinkles along the inside wall of the glass. These will be the ants.

3. MIX some sprinkles into the yogurt. Add a layer of yogurt to the glass. Cover the yogurt layer with more crumbs. Make layers to the top of the glass. The last layer should be crumbs. Add a few sprinkles on top.

4. NOW dig in and eat some ants!

STEVEN TALLEY/TALLEY PHOTO

Name ____________________________

Family: Children will be tested on these spelling words. Have your child read the words, write each word in a box, and cut the boxes apart. Use the word cards for spelling practice throughout the week. Choose a card, say the word, and ask your child to write it.

Spelling List

favor	later	title	equal	broken	human
lazy	final	tiny	secret	total	student

Name ______________________________

Family: Listen to your child read the story a few times this week. With repeated practice, the reading should become smoother and more accurate.

A Big Hit

What's a piñata (say it: peen-YAH-tah)? It's a decoration filled with candy. Friends take turns hitting the piñata with a stick until the candy spills out. You may have been to a piñata party, but it probably wasn't a piñata like this one!

This giant piñata was made for a party in Pennsylvania. It was as tall as a six-story building and held four thousand pounds of candy! A wrecking ball was used to crack the piñata open. Now *that's* what you call a big hit!

ANDY NEWMAN/CARNIVAL CRUISE LINES

Name ______________________________

Family: Have your child find and circle each spelling word in the word-search puzzle and check it off in the list.

Spelling List

- ☐ favor
- ☐ equal
- ☐ lazy
- ☐ secret
- ☐ later
- ☐ broken
- ☐ final
- ☐ total
- ☐ title
- ☐ human
- ☐ tiny
- ☐ student

l	a	z	y	e	f	i	n	a	l
a	r	b	r	o	k	e	n	x	h
t	i	t	l	e	p	l	d	r	s
e	t	o	t	a	l	r	u	p	t
r	i	q	m	z	m	d	h	n	u
o	n	f	a	v	o	r	c	e	d
r	y	e	q	u	a	l	r	i	e
m	t	r	s	e	c	r	e	t	n
h	u	m	a	n	u	w	d	e	t
c	h	i	e	f	i	k	l	t	u

Name ______________________________

Family: Have your child write the missing vowels to complete the spelling words in the puzzles.

a e i o u

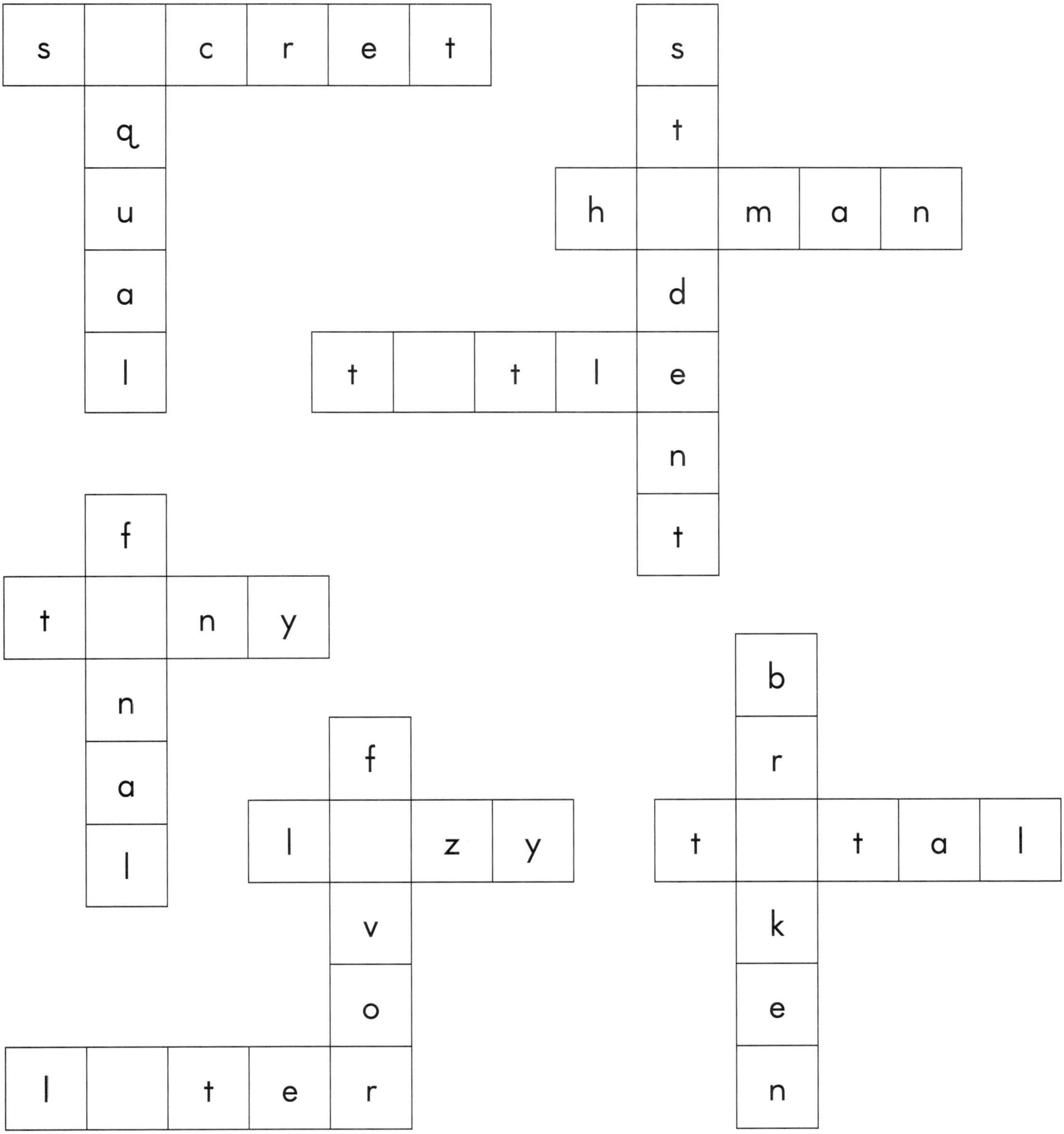

Name ______________________________

Family: Children will be tested on these spelling words. Have your child read the words, write each word in a box, and cut the boxes apart. Use the word cards for spelling practice throughout the week. Choose a card, say the word, and ask your child to write it.

Spelling List

was	wash	were	what	which	whose
want	water	would	where	who	whole

Name ______________________________

Family: Listen to your child read the story a few times this week. Reading should become smoother and more accurate with repeated practice.

A Note for Alec

Alec was sitting on his stool in art class when he felt someone poke him. It was Frits. Frits handed Alec a note, then continued to walk to the pencil sharpener without saying a word.

Alec unfolded the note. It said:

Alec frowned at Frits and shook his head no. Then Alec crumpled the note into a ball and tossed it into the trash can.

"Good shot, Alec!" said Tic. "My team needs a shooter like you. Can you play with us tomorrow?"

Alec's face turned red. "Maybe," he said. Then he looked at Frits with a panicked expression and whispered, "Maybe we <u>should</u> meet after school."

Frits grinned and said, "OK."

Name ______________________________

Family: Have your child read the words on the balls and then write each one in the column that has the sound and spelling that word begins with.

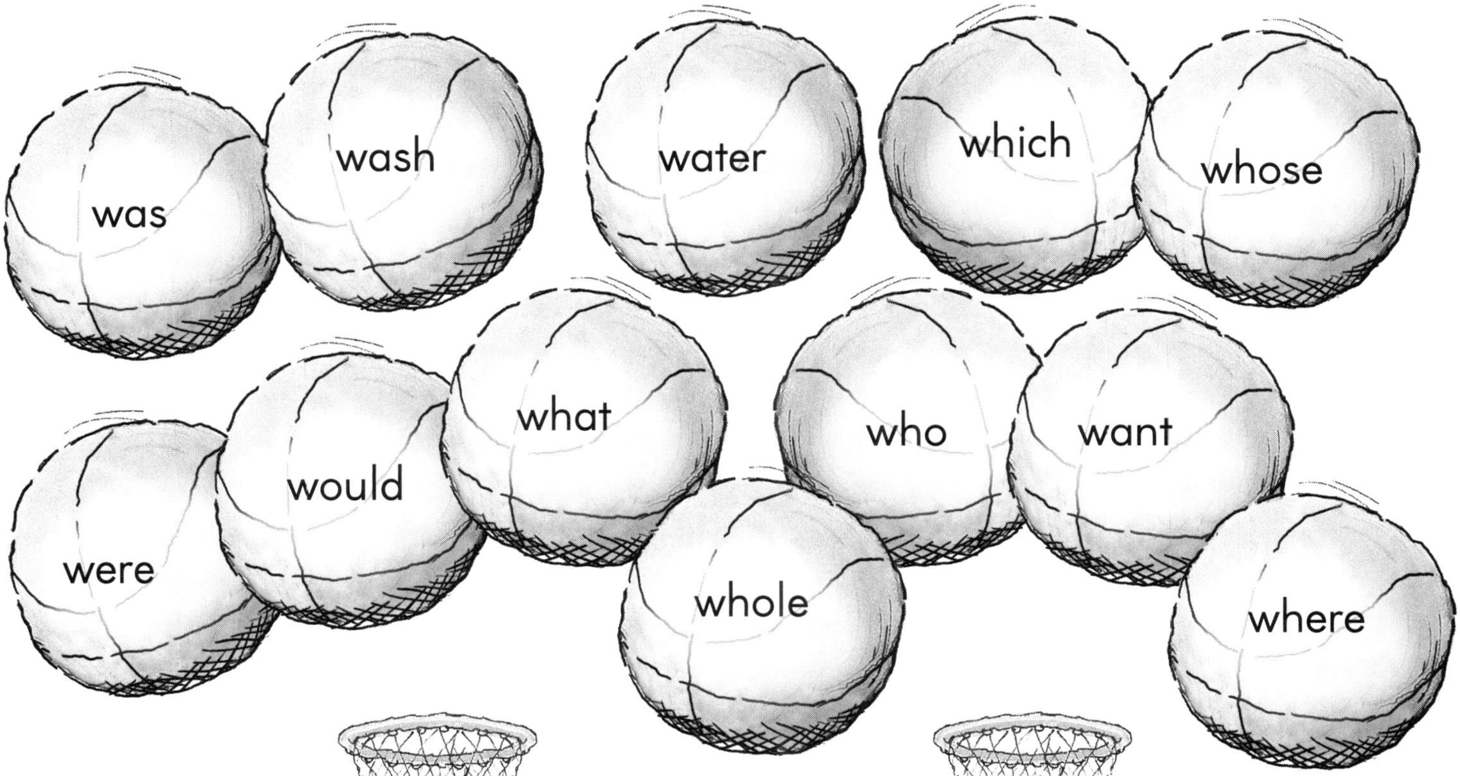

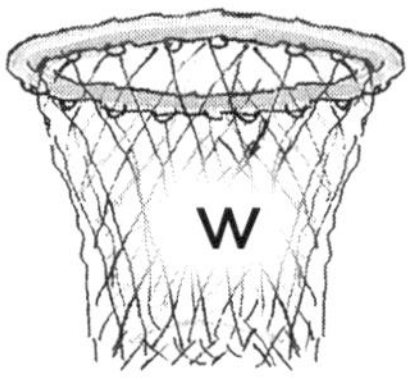

1. ____________________
2. ____________________
3. ____________________
4. ____________________
5. ____________________
6. ____________________

1. ____________________
2. ____________________
3. ____________________
4. ____________________
5. ____________________
6. ____________________

Name ______________________________

Family: Have your child write the spelling word hidden in each group of letters and then write the numbered letters on the lines below to find the answer to the riddle. Hint: Each spelling word begins with *w*.

1. t w h e r e m ___ ___ ___ ___ ___ (1)
2. b w h o v ___ ___ ___
3. h w a n t p ___ ___ ___ ___ (2)
4. s w o u l d f ___ ___ ___ ___ ___
5. c w h i c h e ___ ___ ___ ___ ___
6. g w a t e r h ___ ___ ___ ___ ___ (3)
7. b w a s g ___ ___ ___
8. m w h a t e ___ ___ ___ ___
9. t w h o s e k ___ ___ ___ ___ ___ (4)
10. s e w a s h r ___ ___ ___ ___
11. p w e r e s ___ ___ ___ ___ (5)
12. r w h o l e g ___ ___ ___ ___ ___

What runs but has no legs? Answer: ___ ___ ___ ___ ___ !
1 2 3 4 5

Name ______________________________

Family: Children will be tested on these spelling words. Have your child read the words, write each word in a box, and cut the boxes apart. Use the word cards for spelling practice throughout the week. Choose a card, say the word, and ask your child to write it.

Spelling List

someone something anyone everybody everything nowhere
somewhere anybody anything everyone no one nothing

Name ______________________________

Family: Listen to your child read the story a few times this week. Reading should become smoother and more accurate with repeated practice.

Thursday

Mr. Kumasi taped a map of Africa to the board so everybody could see.

The Superkids looked at one another. This was not the way Ms. Blossom began the day.

Icky said politely, "Ms. Blossom always begins with reading."

"Does she?" said Mr. Kumasi. "Well, today we'll do something different. Watch and listen."

Mr. Kumasi pointed to the map. "I'm from Ghana," he said. "In Ghana, children are often named for the day of the week on which they were born." He wrote the days of the week on the board in big letters. "Everyone, please come stand under your day."

"What if we don't know what day we were born on?" asked Sal.

"Then look at the calendar, and use the day your birthday is <u>this</u> year," said Mr. Kumasi.

The Superkids felt discombobulated. They tripped over one another as they went to the board.

"This is weird!" Tic whispered.

"Yes," giggled Tac. "But I like being Thursday."

Name ______________________________

Family: Help your child find three compound words that have the same first word in a straight or diagonal line. Have your child draw a line through the words and write them on the lines below the Tic-Tac-Toe puzzles.

anybody	afternoon	annoy
anything	angry	airport
anyone	asleep	animal

1. ____________________
2. ____________________
3. ____________________

nowhere	note	never
noise	nothing	north
noontime	none	no one

1. ____________________
2. ____________________
3. ____________________

seafood	someone	sound
sunflower	something	sing
shore	somewhere	snowball

1. ____________________
2. ____________________
3. ____________________

evening	earring	everything
eating	even	everyone
event	endless	everybody

1. ____________________
2. ____________________
3. ____________________

Name ______________________________

Family: Have your child form compound words by tracing each gray word and completing it with the word from the box above the lines. The activity includes this week's spelling words, plus a few extra.

one

1. some ____________
2. any ____________
3. every ____________

body

8. any ____________
9. every ____________
10. some ____________

thing

4. some ____________
5. every ____________
6. no ____________
7. any ____________

where

11. some ____________
12. any ____________
13. no ____________
14. every ____________

Name ______________________________

Family: Children will be tested on these spelling words. Have your child read the words, write each word in a box, and cut the boxes apart. Use the word cards for spelling practice throughout the week. Choose a card, say the word, and ask your child to write it.

Spelling List

breeze	queen	repeat	leave	brief	relief
squeeze	green	defeat	scream	thief	belief

Name ____________________________

Family: Listen to your child read the article a few times this week. With repeated practice, the reading should become smoother and more accurate.

Mud Madness

What do you get when you mix lots of water and tons of dirt? Just add a thousand kids and you'll have Mud Day. It's the day when kids in one Michigan town get to play in a giant puddle of mud. Kids have wheelbarrow races in the muck too. The muddiest boy and girl are crowned Mr. and Ms. Mud. Afterward, everyone gets sprayed clean with a fire hose.

BILL PUGLIANO/GETTY IMAGES

Name ______________________________

Family: Have your child read the spelling words in the box and use the letters in the boxes below to complete each word on the lines. See number 1 as an example. Have your child check off each completed word to make sure the word is on the list and correctly spelled. Use each word only once.

Spelling List

☐ breeze	☐ queen	☐ repeat	☐ leave	☐ brief	☐ relief
☐ squeeze	☐ green	☐ defeat	☐ scream	☐ thief	☐ belief

g u z q n e b r s

r f v c e l p t m

1. q u e e n
2. _ _ _ e e _ _
3. _ _ e e _
4. _ _ e e _ _
5. d _ _ e a _
6. _ e a _ _
7. _ _ _ e a _
8. s _ _ e a _

t h e r b l f

9. b _ _ i e _
10. _ _ i e _
11. t _ i e _
12. _ _ _ i e _

Name ______________________________

Family: Have your child complete two spelling words to match each clue. The first answer is provided. The two words will have the same long *a* spelling in them.

Spelling List

breeze	queen	repeat	leave	brief	relief
squeeze	green	defeat	scream	thief	belief

1. What do you call a tight place that a wind goes through?

a b__________________ s__________________

2. What do you call a loss that happens again?

a r__________________ d__________________

3. What do you call a robber who steals something quickly?

a t__________________ who is b__________________

4. What do you call a ruler who is painted the color of grass?

a g__________________ q__________________

5. What feeling do people have when they know help is coming?

a b__________________ in r__________________

6. What do scared ghosts do in a spooky house?

s__________________ and l__________________

Name ______________________________

Family: Have your child read the recipe. You can then follow the directions to make the snack together.

Sea Monster

You will need:

- a bowl
- a spoon
- whipped cream cheese
- blue food coloring
- a dinner plate
- mini bagels
- a knife
- raisins
- fish-shaped crackers

1. IN a bowl, mix half of the cream cheese with a few drops of food coloring. Spread the mixture on a plate. This will be the water for your sea monster.

2. CUT a mini bagel in half to make two half circles. Put one half aside. Cut the other half in two as shown.

3. PUT the large half of the bagel cut-side down in the center of the plate. Place the smaller pieces of the bagel as shown.

4. USE dabs of cream cheese to stick two raisins on the head for eyes. Place crackers in the blue cream cheese.

STEVEN TALLEY/TALLEY PHOTO

5. Share your snack with your friends. Dip bagels into the cream cheese. Sea monsters are tasty!

Name ______________________________

Family: Children will be tested on these spelling words. Have your child read the words, write each word in a box, and cut the boxes apart. Use the word cards for spelling practice throughout the week. Choose a card, say the word, and ask your child to write it.

Spelling List

steak	break	holiday	stain	explain	cable
great	stay	yesterday	plain	table	fable

Name ______________________________

Family: Listen to your child read the article a few times this week. With repeated practice, the reading should become smoother and more accurate.

In the Swim

A deserted island in the Bahamas is home to a whole herd of wild pigs. These pigs don't wallow in the mud. They live on a beautiful beach where they splash in the surf and nap in the sand. Don't worry. The pigs don't hog the beach. They are friendly and happily swim with people who visit the island.

TRAVIS ROWAN/ALAMY STOCK PHOTO

Name ______________________________

Family: All of this week's spelling words have the long *a* sound. Have your child find and circle each long *a* word in the puzzle and check it off in the list.

Spelling List

- ☐ steak
- ☐ stain
- ☐ great
- ☐ plain
- ☐ break
- ☐ explain
- ☐ stay
- ☐ table
- ☐ holiday
- ☐ cable
- ☐ yesterday
- ☐ fable

brief	stall	holly	hold	holiday	storm	seem	plow	cube
bring	steam	call	stay	hole	stain	please	store	sting
bike	breeze	break	cable	yesterday	fable	plain	pine	expect
strike	great	green	cube	yes	feel	plump	explain	exit
steak	street	scream	bread	yelled	fumble	cab	tall	table

Name ______________________________

Family: Have your child read the words on the raindrops, draw lines between the words that have the same spelling for the long *a* sound, and then write each word in the row with the long *a* spelling that's in the word.

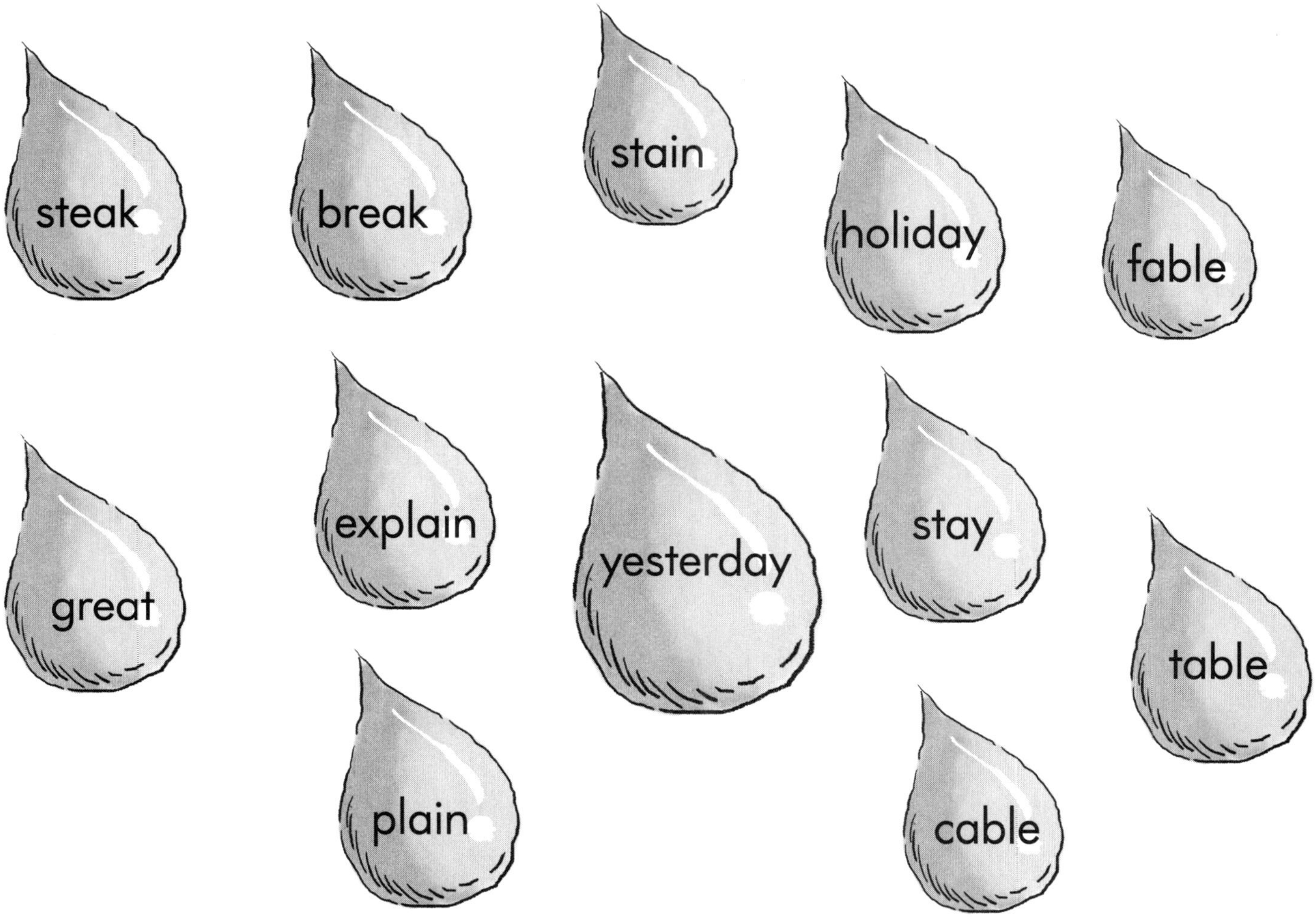

ea 1. ____________ 2. ____________ 3. ____________

ay 4. ____________ 5. ____________ 6. ____________

ai 7. ____________ 8. ____________ 9. ____________

able 10. ____________ 11. ____________ 12. ____________

Name ________________________________

Family: Children will be tested on these spelling words. Have your child read the words, write each word in a box, and cut the boxes apart. Use the word cards for spelling practice throughout the week. Choose a card, say the word, and ask your child to write it.

Spelling List

by	reply	quite	quiet	idea	sign
sky	white	polite	buy	eye	island

Name ____________________________

Family: Listen to your child read the story a few times this week. Reading should become smoother and more accurate with repeated practice.

Ms. Blossom's Idea

Cass met with Ms. Blossom to discuss her paragraph about popcorn. "The best popcorn is at Roosters Field," said Cass. "Everyone will have some at Oswald's party. But I can't go."

"Ah, yes," said Ms. Blossom. "You're hiking instead."

"I wish I weren't," said Cass. "I really want to go to Oswald's party. Do you think I could tell Ana and Oswald that I've changed my mind?"

"No," said Ms. Blossom. "Once you say no to an invitation, that's that."

"Well," replied Cass. "I wasn't quite telling the truth when I said that Ana had <u>already</u> invited me to go hiking."

"Not quite telling the truth is lying, and lying always leads to trouble," said Ms. Blossom.

Cass nodded miserably.

"You can't go to Oswald's party," said Ms. Blossom. "But you're still his friend. Maybe you could find a way to show him that you're happy it's his birthday."

"Thanks," said Cass as she gave Ms. Blossom a hug.

Name ______________________________

Family: Have your child read the spelling words in the lists and then put each list in ABC order on the lines below.

List 1

sign	buy
white	idea
quiet	polite

1. ____________________
2. ____________________
3. ____________________
4. ____________________
5. ____________________
6. ____________________

List 2

island	eye
quite	reply
by	sky

1. ____________________
2. ____________________
3. ____________________
4. ____________________
5. ____________________
6. ____________________

Name ______________________________

Family: Have your child use the spelling words to complete the sentences.

Spelling List

by	reply	quite	quiet	idea	sign
sky	white	polite	buy	eye	island

1. Snow is __________________ and the ____________________ is blue.

2. Kids with good manners are ______________________________.

3. The opposite of sell is ______________ .

4. Something that is next to you is _________________________ you.

5. When you add silent *e* to quit, you make _____________________.

6. Ask a question and get a ______________________ .

7. To get an _______________________, you must think.

8. The opposite of loud is ________________________ .

9. Your ____________________________ helps you to see.

10. A stop _______________ tells cars to stop.

11. You need a boat to get to an ____________________ .

Name ______________________________

Family: Children will be tested on these spelling words. Have your child read the words, write each word in a box, and cut the boxes apart. Use the word cards for spelling practice throughout the week. Choose a card, say the word, and ask your child to write it.

Spelling List

groan	charcoal	stone	ocean	clothes	sew
croak	zone	rewrote	both	close	so

Name ______________________________

Family: Listen to your child read the story a few times this week. Reading should become smoother and more accurate with repeated practice.

Enjoy the Cookie

The next day, Sal was leaving the lunch table when Ettabetta said, "Wait."

"Now what?" groaned Sal.

"Dessert!" said Ettabetta. She handed Sal a homemade chocolate-chip cookie.

"Thanks!" said Sal. He sat back down.

Sal started to eat, but Ettabetta said, "Not so fast!" She took out paper and a pencil. "First tell me how the cookie looks."

"It's golden-brown," said Sal.

Ettabetta wrote golden brown. "Now take a bite," she said. "Don't rush. Think, then tell me how the cookie tastes and feels."

Sal chewed slowly, then said, "I never noticed this before, but the cookie part is soft and sweet, and the chip part is hard and a little bitter."

"Great!" said Ettabetta, writing down Sal's words. "How does it smell?"

"Chocolatey," he sighed happily.

"Excellent!" said Ettabetta. "You knew what to write all along. You just needed to slow down and enjoy the cookie!"

Name ___________________________________

Family: Sal left something out of some of his cookies. Have your child cross out the cookies with the words that do not have the long *o* sound, as in home.

Spelling List

groan	charcoal	stone	ocean	clothes	sew
croak	zone	rewrote	both	close	so

Name ___________________________

Family: Have your child write the spelling words that fit the clues.

Spelling List

groan	charcoal	stone	ocean	clothes	sew
croak	zone	rewrote	both	close	so

1. I rhyme with moan. I am a sad noise. ______________
2. I rhyme with growth. I am two things together. ______________
3. I rhyme with soak. I am a noise a frog makes. ______________
4. My second syllable rhymes with goal. ______________
5. I rhyme with rose. I am what you wear. ______________
6. I rhyme with bone. I am a special place. ______________
7. I rhyme with no. I mean the same as stitch. ______________
8. I have a prefix. I mean to write again. ______________
9. I rhyme with cone. I mean the same as rock. ______________
10. I rhyme with nose. I am the opposite of open. ______________
11. I rhyme with motion. I mean the same as sea. ______________
12. I rhyme with go. I mean the same as very. ______________

Name ______________________________

Family: Children will be tested on these spelling words. Have your child read the words, write each word in a box, and cut the boxes apart. Use the word cards for spelling practice throughout the week. Choose a card, say the word, and ask your child to write it.

Spelling List

fruit	blue	soup	loop	blew	rule
juice	glue	group	food	grew	rude

Name ______________________________

Family: Listen to your child read the article a few times this week. With repeated practice, the reading should become smoother and more accurate.

Wigging Out

Hundreds of years ago, people thought it was stylish to have really big hair. Rich people often had the biggest hair because they could buy large, fancy wigs. Those people were called "big wigs." Today, you don't need huge hair to be called a bigwig. You just have to be important.

ARCHIVES CHARMET/THE BRIDGEMAN ART LIBRARY

Name ____________________

Family: Have your child draw a straight or diagonal line through the three words in each puzzle that have the long *oo* sound as in soon, and then write the words on the lines below puzzle.

fruit	free	supper
blue	fit	black
soup	soap	but

1. ____________________
2. ____________________
3. ____________________

roll	blow	loop
lap	rail	blew
blend	lip	rule

1. ____________________
2. ____________________
3. ____________________

grip	glue	glum
rub	group	glad
rod	rude	road

1. ____________________
2. ____________________
3. ____________________

juice	just	junk
feed	food	find
grow	green	grew

1. ____________________
2. ____________________
3. ____________________

Name ______________________________

Family: Have your child subtract and add letters to write a spelling word that solves each word problem. Explain that the new letters should be added in the same place where letters were taken away. The first problem has been completed.

1. chew – ch + bl = blew
2. hoop – h + l = ________________
3. clue – c + b = ________________
4. soap – a + u = ________________
5. nice – n + ju = ________________
6. mood – m + f = ________________
7. true – tr + gl = ________________
8. suit – s + fr = ________________
9. crude – c = ________________
10. grip – i + ou = ________________
11. new – n + gr = ________________
12. mule – m + r = ________________

Name ___________________________

Family: Have your child read the recipe. You can then follow the directions to make the snack together.

Go Bananas

You will need:

- a banana, peeled and sliced
- 2 plates
- wax paper
- toothpicks
- a bowl
- Magic Shell topping
- confetti sprinkles

1. PUT banana slices on a plate with wax paper. Stick a toothpick in the center of each slice. Put the plate in the freezer. When frozen, take the slices out of the freezer.
2. SQUEEZE topping into the bowl. Hold a banana slice by the toothpick. Dip the slice into the topping until it's covered.
3. BEFORE the topping hardens, hold the slice over the other plate and drop sprinkles onto the banana. Set the slice back on the wax paper.

STEVEN TALLEY/TALLEY PHOTO

4. REPEAT the steps with the other slices. Wait for the topping to harden and serve frozen!

Name ______________________________

Family: Children will be tested on these spelling words. Have your child read the words, write each word in a box, and cut the boxes apart. Use the word cards for spelling practice throughout the week. Choose a card, say the word, and ask your child to write it.

Spelling List

fair	fairy	tear	stare	merry	library
stair	dairy	wear	share	ferry	dictionary

Name ______________________________

Family: Listen to your child read the article a few times this week. With repeated practice, the reading should become smoother and more accurate.

Walk on the Wild Side

How would you like a pair of banana boots? Or would you rather loaf in a pair of loafers? If you like to walk barefoot in the grass, you might want sandals with real grass growing from the soles. When it comes to funny footwear, there is no limit to what you can do. What kind of shoes would you wear if you let your feet and your imagination run wild?

Name ______________________________

Family: Have your child write the spelling word that matches each meaning.

Spelling List

fair	fairy	tear	stare	merry	library
stair	dairy	wear	share	ferry	dictionary

1. a magical creature ___ ___ ___ ___ ___

2. to put on clothes ___ ___ ___ ___

3. to give something you have to others ___ ___ ___ ___ ___

4. happy ___ ___ ___ ___ ___

5. a place with many books ___ ___ ___ ___ ___ ___ ___

6. a boat for cars ___ ___ ___ ___ ___

7. following the rules ___ ___ ___ ___

8. a long, hard look ___ ___ ___ ___ ___

9. where milk is made ___ ___ ___ ___ ___

10. a book of word meanings ___ ___ ___ ___ ___ ___ ___ ___ ___ ___

11. to rip ___ ___ ___ ___

12. a step ___ ___ ___ ___ ___

Name ________________________________

Family: Have your child unscramble the spelling word by each number, and then write the word correctly on the line. The spelling list and first letter of each word have been provided for clues.

unscrmable

Spelling List

fair	fairy	tear	stare
merry	library	stair	dairy
wear	share	ferry	dictionary

1. airyf f ____________________
2. meryr m ____________________
3. airts s ____________________
4. etar t ____________________
5. aresh s ____________________
6. arytiondic d ____________________
7. tares s ____________________
8. raew w ____________________
9. rarylib l ____________________
10. airf f ____________________
11. yriad d ____________________
12. efrry f ____________________

Name ______________________________

Family: Children will be tested on these spelling words. Have your child read the words, write each word in a box, and cut the boxes apart. Use the word cards for spelling practice throughout the week. Choose a card, say the word, and ask your child to write it.

Spelling List

worn	wore	door	four	soar	warm
forty	store	floor	pour	board	warn

Name ______________________________

Family: Listen to your child read the story a few times this week. Reading should become smoother and more accurate with repeated practice.

Field Day

Back at school, the Superkids were getting ready for Field Day. They loved Field Day, but this year they were a bit sad as they stood in line waiting to go outside. More than a week had passed, and they still hadn't heard anything from the judges of the America Goes Green Contest. "I guess they're not interested," sighed Lily.

"It would have been fun to surprise Ms. Blossom," said Icky.

"And to be in the parade," added Doc.

Everyone was disappointed. They'd worked so hard on their entry!

But it was hard to stay disappointed once the games began. The day was warm and sunny. The playground was divided into different stations. At each station, there was something fun to do. Just about everything was wonderfully wet and messy!

Name ________________________________

Family: Have your child show the Superkids' path through the Field Day stations by drawing a line connecting all the words with the *or* sound as in more.

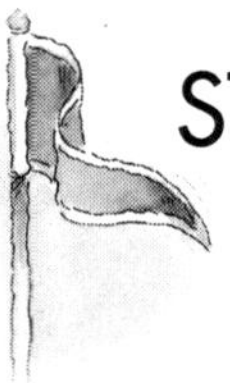

START

store pour worn bird

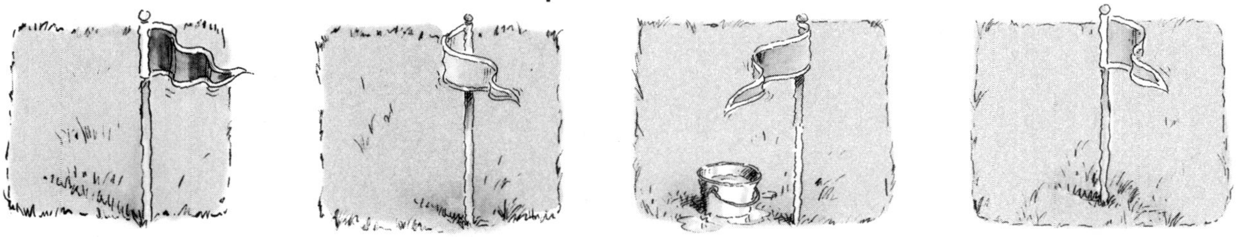

deer stare door worm

floor warn board barn

forty wore wire farm

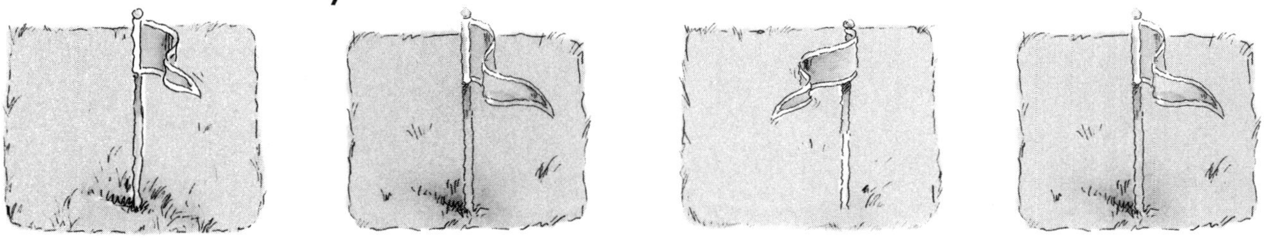

party soar warm four

FINISH!

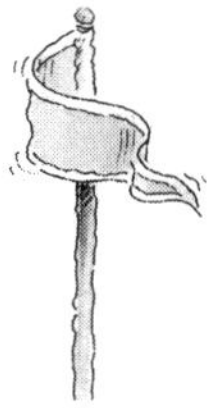

Name ______________________________

Family: Have your child read the spelling words at the top of the page, then unscramble the words and write each word correctly on the line. The first letter of each word has been provided.

unscrmable

Spelling List

worn	wore	door	four
soar	warm	forty	store
floor	pour	board	warn

1. ourf f____________________
2. arwm w____________________
3. aodrb b____________________
4. onrw w____________________
5. pruo p____________________
6. doro d____________________
7. rotfy f____________________
8. reow w____________________
9. arso s____________________
10. loorf f____________________
11. tores s____________________
12. arnw w____________________

Name ______________________________

Family: Children will be tested on these spelling words. Have your child read the words, write each word in a box, and cut the boxes apart. Use the word cards for spelling practice throughout the week. Choose a card, say the word, and ask your child to write it.

Spelling List

stir	desert	burn	doctor	earn	collar
birthday	dessert	Thursday	motor	search	forward

Name ______________________________

Family: Listen to your child read the story a few times this week. Reading should become smoother and more accurate with repeated practice.

Tired, Lonely, and Sad

And where was Golly? He was walking down a sidewalk next to a busy road. He had found his way to town, but he was just as lost as ever. Cars swished past, blowing grit and dust in his eyes. His paws were sore, and his legs were tired. But Golly walked on until at last the sun began to set. Then he collapsed in a heap next to a dumpster.

As the sky became darker and the streetlights went on, Golly felt more and more lonely and sad. He missed the safe, warm barn. He missed the horses' gentle breathing. He missed the owls' soft hooting and the sheep sighing in their sleep.

Here in town, it was never quiet. Cars honked and sirens blared. Often, Golly heard music, and people laughing and talking and calling out to one another. But he never heard anyone calling out to him.

Golly curled up and rested his nose on his paws. He was tired, hungry, thirsty, and lost. But Golly was brave and determined. As soon as the sun rose, he would continue his search for the Superkids. And he wouldn't stop until he found them.

Name ______________________________

Family: Have your child write the missing spelling word to complete each phrase.

Spelling List

stir	desert	burn	doctor	earn	collar
birthday	dessert	Thursday	motor	search	forward

1. s ______________________
to mix

2. T ______________________
or Friday

3. e ______________________
money

4. b ______________________
present

5. f ______________________
or backward

6. d ______________________
and nurse

7. d ______________________
sands

8. m ______________________
boat

9. c ______________________
for a dog

10. s ______________________
and find

11. b ______________________
wood in a fire

12. d ______________________
comes after dinner

Name ______________________________

Family: Have your child write the spelling word hidden in each group of letters and then write the numbered letters on the lines below to find out who Golly was trying to find.

Spelling List

stir	desert	burn	doctor	earn	collar
birthday	dessert	Thursday	motor	search	forward

1. S T h u r s d a y M ___ ___ ___ ___ ___ ___ ___ ___ (1)
2. n i b i r t h d a y n ___ ___ ___ ___ ___ ___ ___ ___ (2)
3. t d e s e r t h ___ ___ ___ ___ ___ ___ (3)
4. s c o l l a r k ___ ___ ___ ___ ___ ___
5. W S e a r c h S ___ ___ ___ ___ ___ ___ (4)
6. a b u r n l y ___ ___ ___ ___ (5)
7. Q U d o c t o r c ___ ___ ___ ___ ___ ___
8. t e a r n g ___ ___ ___ ___ (6)
9. s m o t o r o l ___ ___ ___ ___ ___ (7)
10. K s t i r t ___ ___ ___ ___ (8)
11. C h f o r w a r d p ___ ___ ___ ___ ___ ___ ___ (9)
12. d d e s s e r t t ___ ___ ___ ___ ___ ___ ___ (10)

Answer: ___ ___ ___ ___ ___ p ___ ___ k ___ ___ ___ !
(1 2 3 4 5 p 6 7 k 8 9 10)